How to Put On a
Great Craft Show--
First Time and Every Time!

Second Edition

by Dianne Hendricks Spiegel, Lee Spiegel, and A. B. Petrow

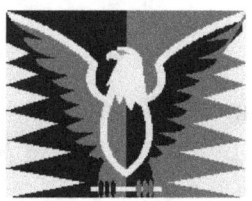

Craftmasters™ Books
Sebastopol, California

Disclaimer
This publication is designed to provide accurate and authoritative information with regard to the subject matter covered. It is sold with the understanding that the Publisher is not engaged in rendering legal, accounting, or other professional advice. If legal advice or other expert assistance is required, the services of a competent professional person should be sought.
--From a Declaration of Principles jointly adopted by a Committee of the American Bar Association and a Committee of Publishers and Associations.

Every effort has been made to make this book as complete and as accurate as possible, but no warranty or fitness is implied. Neither the author nor Craftmasters Books and Videos, nor anyone else who has been involved in the creation, production, or delivery of this product shall be liable for any direct, incidental or consequential damages, such as, but not limited to, loss of anticipated profits or benefits, resulting from its use or from any breach of any warranty. Some states do not allow the exclusion or limitation of direct, incidental or consequential damages so the above limitation may not apply to you.

This book was produced with Microsoft **Word** from Microsoft Corp. **Windows** is a registered trademark of Microsoft Corporation. All other product and brand names mentioned in this publication are trademarks or registered trademarks of their respective holders.

Acknowledgments
Second edition edited by (and appendix I-III written by) A. B. Petrow.
Thanks to Cynthia Ellis for her very generous help in editing and proofreading.

Original ISBN 0-9629897-2-X. Original Library of Congress Number: 91-65843

Second Edition:

ISBN-13: 978-0-9655193-8-0
ISBN-10: 0-9655193-8-4

Printed in USA by printingsystem.com

Photos by A. B. Petrow

Cover photo "Art in the Park," Boulder City, Nevada

Dedication

Dedicated to the thousands of wonderful artists and craftspeople we've met during the last two decades, and to those caring promoters who have helped them find an appreciative buying public.

> *--Lee and Dianne Spiegel*

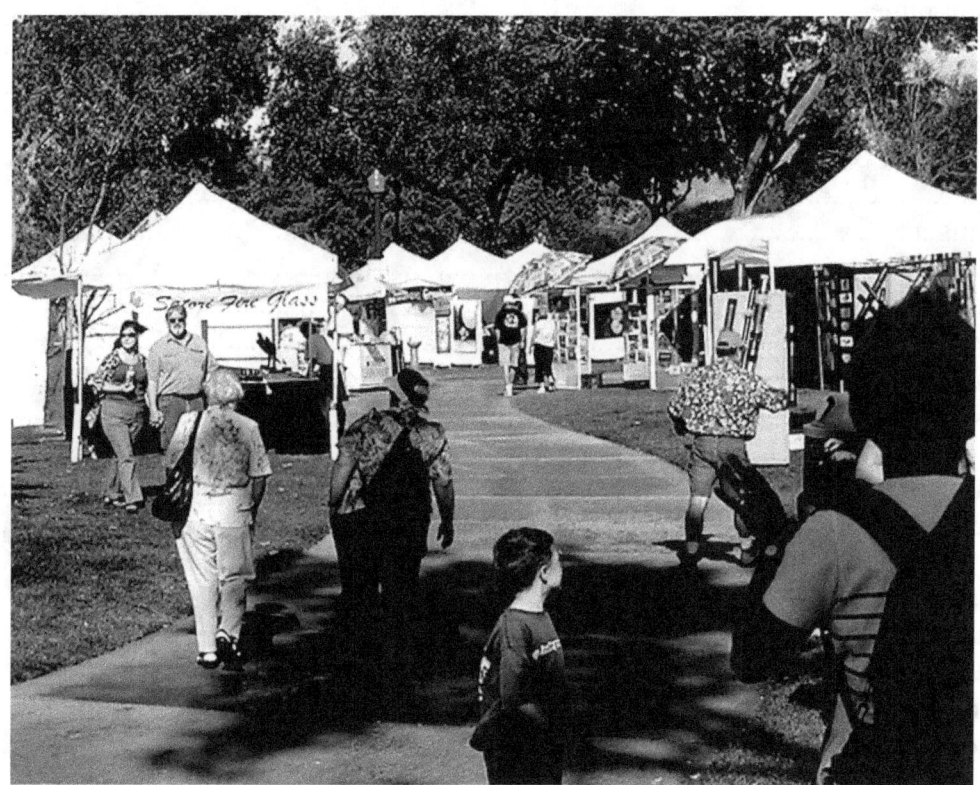

Art in the Park, Any Town, USA

Contents

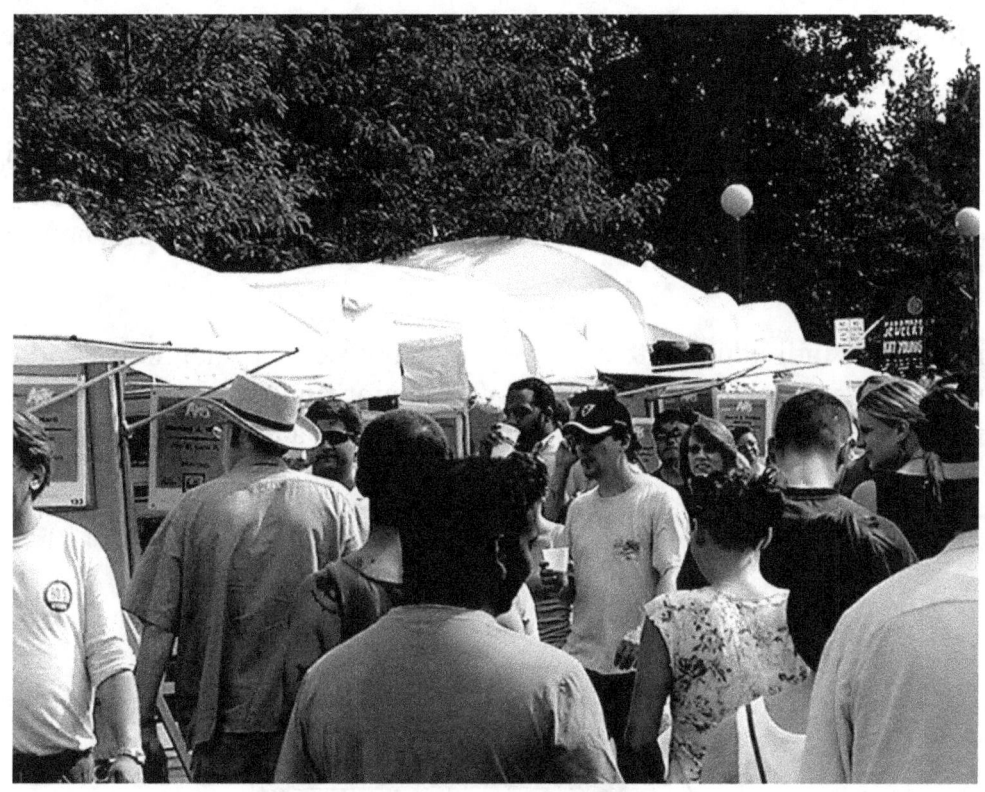

Columbus Arts Festival, Columbus, Ohio

Introduction

What an exciting time to begin planning a crafts fair in your community! Public interest in handmade arts and crafts has never been higher. The crafts fair movement, which came into its own in the 1960s, shows no signs of abating. In fact, it seems to grow stronger each year.

Craft shows, fairs, and festivals have become a staple of community life and run the gamut from small, individually-produced, single-focus shows to large, professionally-produced annual events with gross receipts in the millions of dollars. (Figures 1 and 2 illustrate the theoretical differences between a small "show" and a large "fair" or "festival." In actuality, these terms are often used interchangeably.)

Members of the public happily return to good shows year after year, supporting their favorite craftspeople and looking for unusual and innovative work. Badly produced, sloppily done, or insufficiently advertised shows are largely ignored and wither away, as well they should!

Successful crafts shows can be simple or elaborate, making it possible for individuals and/or groups with varied human and material resources to sponsor them. In the pages that follow, we will discuss the many aspects of successful craft show, fair, and festival production.

Whether you're an individual with a desire to promote a small neighborhood craft show, or a member of a large organization with major fund-raising interests, this book can set you on the right path and help you sponsor a memorable event.

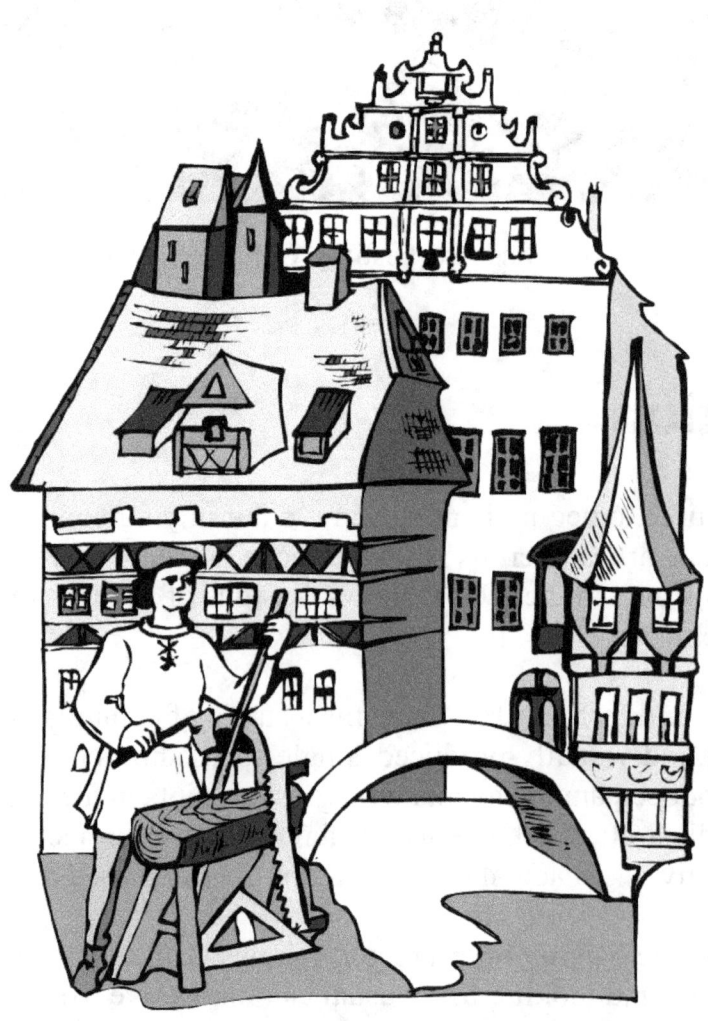

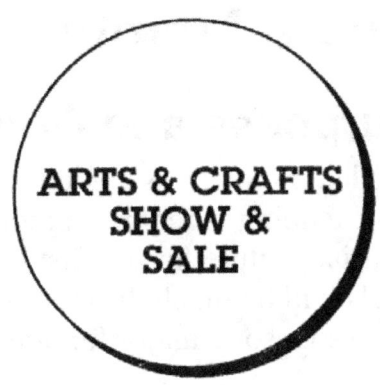

Figure 1: The Single-Focus Craft Show

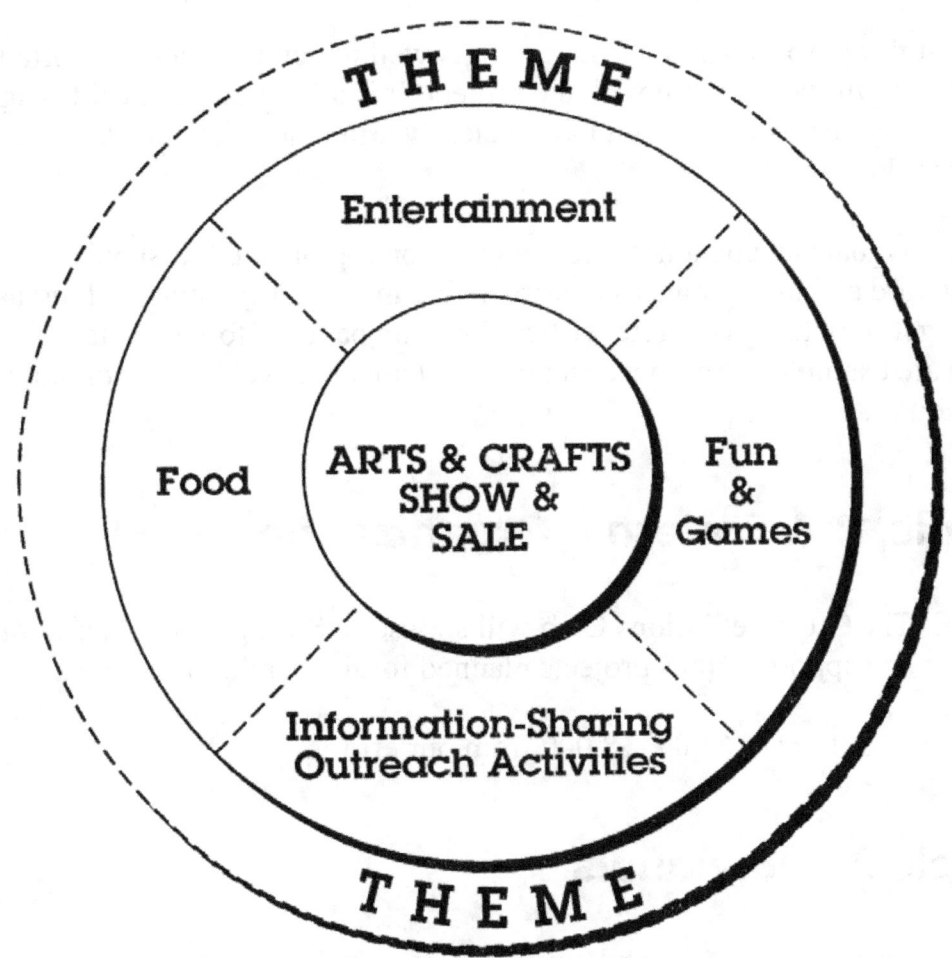

Figure 2: The Multiple-Focus Craft Fair/Festival

PART 1: Planning a Memorable Event

Identifying Your Purposes and Goals

Before embarking on any complex project, it is a good idea to give serious thought to the hows and whys of what you're doing. Are you an individual with limited resources trying an entrepreneurial venture for the first time? Good for you! Obviously, your needs and goals will be much different from those of a large fraternal organization seeking to sponsor a major fundraising event.

Sit down and give some thought to who you are, what resources are available to you, and exactly what you hope to accomplish through your efforts. Develop a statement of purpose and a tentative goal.

Be sure that this purpose and goal statement is well understood and supported by everyone who will be involved with the project. It is a lot easier to avoid snags, pitfalls, and arguments later if you have a clearly articulated statement of what you are trying to do.

Your purpose/goal statement need not be fancy or complicated. It should be straightforward and as accurate as possible. You may modify your thinking as you go along, but get something concrete written down on paper before you start. The following are examples of purpose and goal statements developed by organizations and individuals.

Example 1: A Fraternal Organization

PURPOSE: The Greenfield Lions Club will sponsor a Spring Crafts Fair in order to raise money to support various projects planned for the coming fiscal year.

GOAL: We want to net $6,000 -$8,000 from our efforts.

Example 2: Individuals

PURPOSE: Jane Smith and Sarah Brown will pool their crafts knowledge and organize a boutique-type craft sale at the Community Center for the purpose of generating some extra income for themselves and other craftswomen in the community.

GOAL: For Jane and Sarah, to net at least $1,000 this year and to begin working toward promoting an annual event celebrating community craftswomen. For participating craftswomen, to show a profit and enhance self esteem.

Example 3: Church

PURPOSE: Saint John's Church must raise $20,000 this year in order to provide continued support to its Mission in Paraguay.

GOAL: We will net one-third ($6,700) of our annual operating revenues by sponsoring a community crafts fair to be held on Church property.

Example 4: Community Organization

PURPOSE: The purpose of sponsoring a Festival is to support the work of the Back Bay Main Street Improvement Association, particularly to provide revenue for the replanting of Main Street's median strip.

GOAL: We will raise $20,000 each year for the next three years by sponsoring and supporting a repeated community event.

As you can see, purpose and goal statements can vary widely.

Secondary Goals

If indicated, you can also list secondary purposes or goals such as:

- to increase community awareness of our group and its work,

- to develop group cohesiveness and a sense of common purpose,

- to develop ties with other organizations in the community,

- to recruit new members,

- to provide the community with an enjoyable social event,

- to support the arts and the talented craftspeople living in the area.

Time Line

In the best of all possible worlds, you will give yourself about one year to plan a first-time event. This is ideal rather than absolute. In no case, however, should you give yourself less than six months' preparation time. Planning a craft show is not unlike planning a large, elaborate wedding. If you want either one to come off without major glitches, planning will be complex and time consuming. Start by selecting a show length and considering some possible dates.

Time Frame

About 98 percent of all crafts fairs occur on weekends (Saturday and/or Sunday) or three-day weekends (Friday through Sunday). Since some of the "lesser" holidays have been moved to Mondays, there are a number of large shows that now take advantage of the Saturday-Monday holiday combination, particularly Memorial Day, Labor Day, and, in the south, Presidents' Day.

There are a few days or weekends you should probably eliminate right off the bat. The weekends before Christmas and New Year's Day come immediately to mind. And, unless you live in a sunbelt state, the months of January, February, and March will probably not attract the size crowds you'd like to have at your show.

Show Length

Your first effort will probably be a one- or a two-day event. According to a survey by Claire V. Dorst (see Reference List), the two-day show length is overwhelmingly preferred by exhibiting craftspersons. On the other hand, you may feel more comfortable planning a one-day show as an initial effort.

Let's look at the relative merits of each.

The One Day Show

Advantages

1. May be less stressful for a first-time promoter

2. May be slightly less expensive to mount

3. Will not require overnight security

4 Will require fewer manpower hours

5. Exhibitors from out of town will not incur overnight lodging expenses.

Disadvantages

1. No opportunity to correct first-day errors or problems

2. Competition (for craftspeople) with two-day shows in the area

3. Lower sales revenues for craftspeople

4. Lower sponsor income

5. Possibility of a total rain-out for an outdoor show

The Two-Day Show

Advantages

1. Easier to attract serious professional craftspeople

2. Can correct first-day errors or problems overnight

3. It takes only about 25% more effort and expense to mount a two-day show which can generate 100% more income.

4. Most of the major work is done on the first day. The second day can be a lot easier.

5. Can take advantage of the contemplative shopper (AKA the Be-Backer!)

6. In case of rain on the first day, the second day may prevent a total rain-out.

Disadvantages

1. Arrangements for security will be needed, requiring additional money and/or manpower.

2. Outdoor toilets will have to be pumped out.

3. Area will need cleaning each day.

4. Possibly more expensive (particularly if renting a hall or other large indoor site)

5. Possibly more manpower will be needed.

Saturday or Sunday?

If you decide to mount a one-day show, it might not make much difference, in terms of sales and attendance, whether you pick Saturday or Sunday, but the customs of your community should be considered. What do people do on weekends in your town? If everyone goes to church on Sundays and then spends the day visiting relatives, it may be better to have any one-day shows on Saturday.

Dates

Having decided on a one- or a two-day show, consider dates. The most important thing to bear in mind is competition from conflicting events.

Woe to the sponsor who inadvertently schedules a show on the third day of the World Series, especially if strong local sentiments are involved! The same might go for homecoming in a college town, or a huge, prestigious art show in a neighboring city.

To make sure this doesn't happen to you, check the events calendars in local newspapers, consult local trade papers and magazines (see Resource List), and contact the Chamber of Commerce. Find out what's going on in your area, and use the data to make a good scheduling decision.

Nationwide, most shows take place from April to December. Spring shows can be pleasant, although the weather is often uncertain. Summer shows may take advantage of an influx of tourists and good weather conditions. Fall shows appeal to holiday shoppers looking for unusual gift items. There is no right answer here.

Choosing a Site

Much will depend on the conditions and personality of your own particular community.

Successful crafts fairs occur in many types of settings. Choosing a good site is an important task which should be given thoughtful consideration.

Outdoor Shows

Outdoor shows have much to recommend them. The public can enjoy fresh air, natural scenery, and the opportunity to view arts and crafts in an attractive setting. There is usually more space for booths and walkways, kids can romp around without causing serious problems, and food and entertainment can generally be more extensive.

Outdoor sites such as community parks are often available for little or no money. This can be a real help when you're trying to hold down expenses.

On the other hand, bad weather can destroy an outdoor show and, if you live in an area where precipitation or high winds are year-around possibilities, you might not want the added stress of worrying about what the weather has in store for show day.

Security is also more difficult at outdoor events and, with a show of any size, you'll have the expense of contracting for portable toilets.

Indoor Shows

Indoor shows generally offer a higher level of control for promoters. There will be less worry over weather conditions, sanitary facilities, and overnight security.

It is possible to have a show which occurs outdoors but offers protection from the elements. A tented or canopied area for crafts is one possibility; the overhangs or awnings on some buildings in strip shopping centers is another.

Possible Sites

Following are lists of possible fair sites you might want to consider.

Outdoor

- Parks

- Fairgrounds

- Along city sidewalks

- In streets, closed to vehicular traffic

- In walkways or in parking lots at shopping centers

- On lawns of community or private buildings (club houses, wineries, historic mansions, art centers, YMCAs, etc.)

- Beach parking lots

- School or church grounds

- College quads

- Industrial parks

Indoor

- Church halls or basements

- School gymnasiums or multi-purpose rooms

- Community centers or historic buildings

- Convention centers

- Halls of fraternal organizations

- Fairground exhibit halls

- Meeting rooms and ballrooms at hotels or motels

- Enclosed shopping malls

- Art centers

- Vacant buildings or stores

Mixed:

- Strip shopping centers under building overhangs or awnings

- Buildings and surrounding lawns and parking lots

- Tented or canopied display areas

- Covered stalls at fairgrounds

Location, Size, and Access

No matter what type of site you select, attention should be paid to all of the following items:

An ideal site will be centrally located and not too far off the beaten path, easy to find, and in a pleasant, safe area of town.

The site should be large enough to accommodate the number of exhibitor spaces you want and need to realize a profitable show.

Members of the public and exhibiting crafts persons should have easy access to the facility. Sites with steep flights of stairs, narrow, winding, dark streets, uneven terrain, and other environmental impediments are often bad choices.

Support Services

For an indoor show, you will need a building that provides adequate lighting and electrical hook-ups, ample restroom facilities, an on-site concessionaire (or room to establish your own food services), and good parking facilities.

If setting up an outdoor show, good parking, restroom facilities, and food services will also be necessary.

Cost

Renting a large indoor facility could be a real budget buster. Look for sites with reasonable (or no) rental fees. Check with Chambers of Commerce, parks and recreation departments, community groups, and shopping malls in your area. Also, talk with active, involved friends and acquaintances. Someone you know may have access to just the site you're looking for. You never know who has what community connections until you ask!

Permits

Unless you own the site where you hold your show, you'll need someone's permission to use it. According to John Goodwin (see Reference List), it's a good idea to "make binding arrangements for the rental of show space."

In other words, consider your arrangement to be a short-term lease. Make sure you know what you are renting, how much you are paying, and any special rules that will apply (such as local noise ordinances, rules restricting the sale of alcohol, city licenses to be obtained, etc.). After negotiations are complete, you can draw up an informal contract or letter of agreement spelling out terms. In the rare case of a disagreement, you'll have something in writing to which you can refer.

Insurance

We've found the liability insurance issue to be a real puzzler, and there are many and varied opinions on the subject. If you decide you need insurance, try to get a rider attached to an existing policy. Single-event liability policies can be quite costly. In any case, think critically, ask a lot of questions of people you trust, and shop around. A release-of-liability statement on your application is always a good idea.

The Floor Plan

Every show, indoor and outdoor, will need a floor plan or site map. Once you've selected and measured your site, draw a floor plan, to scale, on a large sheet of cardboard or poster board. Be sure to include all of the impediments on the site (trees, columns, power poles, doorways, windows, etc.) so you'll have an accurate representation of the way things really are.

Plan on allowing 10 x 10 foot spaces for exhibitors' displays, with aisles about 15 feet wide.

There are shows that offer several sizes of spaces (8' x 10', 10'x 12', 10' x 20', etc.) or irregularly shaped spaces, but for your first endeavor, try to keep things as simple and uniform as possible. Most exhibitors are used to working in a 10' x10' space, and their displays have been designed to fit these dimensions.

Remember to keep exhibitors away from fire exits, and do not place displays too close to restroom entrances or food concessions, especially if on-site cooking will occur. Don't forget to plan for a separate eating area with space for tables and chairs or benches.

As you develop your floor plan for an indoor show, check for electrical outlets. Some exhibitors will need electricity; most will not. You will have to let the craftspeople know what you can provide and what they must supply for themselves. You may also want to charge extra for booths with access to electricity.

Number of Exhibitors

When considering how many exhibitors to accept into your show, keep in mind that your objectives are to attract an audience and to make a profit. A show that is too small will not accomplish these objectives. One that is too large will seriously compromise your resources and spread sales over so many exhibitors that none will make much money.

The number of exhibitors you accept should depend on:

1. the number and availability of craftspeople in your area,

2. the human and material resources at your disposal,

3. the size and type of site you select, and

4. the size of your potential audience (population of the immediate area and surrounding towns, tourist traffic, etc.)

There is no firm rule for designating shows as small, medium, or large. But just to give you some type of rough approximation, we'd consider a show to be small if it had 50 or fewer exhibitors, and large with 150 or more. Medium would be somewhere in between.

Setting Exhibitor Fees

The amount you will charge craftspeople to take part in your show will depend on several factors. Your objective will be to generate enough revenue from promoting the show to pay all expenses with enough left over (profit) to have made your efforts worthwhile.

Revenues are generated in several ways:

1. Charging exhibitors an entry fee (flat fee);

2. Charging exhibitors an entry fee plus a percentage of their sales (fee plus percentage - typically 10%);

3. Charging the public to enter the show (admission fee);

4. Selling food and/or beverages directly to the public;

5. Soliciting independent food and beverage vendors and charging them a fee (same as applies to crafts exhibitors, although the fee is usually higher);

6. Offering various revenue-producing games, auctions, drawings, raffles, etc. at your show.

Do a little research before you decide how to set fees. Check local trade papers and magazines (see Resource List) to see who charges what for shows occurring in your vicinity. You will have to stay within the bounds of what is usual, reasonable, and customary in your area in terms of fees. Until you've gained a good reputation, it would be wise to stay at the low end of the scale.

Usually, outdoor shows charge less than indoor shows, and shows with percentage requirements have lower initial entry fees.

Example

To illustrate the preceding points we'll turn to a specific example. A map illustrating this example may be found on page 53.

Let's say that you've decided to mount a one day outdoor show with 75 crafts booths and 10 independent food vendors.

You will charge each craftsperson a $100 entry fee and a 10% commission on sales over $400. (This assures that only the folks who do well will be required to pay the commission.)

Food vendors will be charged $200 plus 10% on total sales.

$100 per booth x 75 booths =	**$7,500**
$200 per food booth x 10 booths =	**$2,000**
Total revenue from flat fees =	**$9,500**

If you fill the show as planned, you are certain of grossing $9,500. If you do a good job with advertising and publicity and attract a good-sized buying crowd, you can be sure of much more when you collect your percentages. For planning and budgeting sake, we'll figure this conservatively as a $12,000 show (estimating $2,500 in commissions from crafts and food booths).

About 50% of the gross will be needed for expenses. Therefore, the total budget for this show will be $6,000. Let's examine how this money should be spent.

Formulating a Budget

For the sake of clarity, we have used the same crafts fair example to illustrate points throughout this book. So let's look at the projected budget for:

The Hill Valley Springtime Fair

Projected Income 75 crafts booths @ $100 ea.	$7,500
10 food booths @ $200 ea.	$2,000
Projected from booth percentages (a very conservative figure)	$2,500
	Total $12,000
Show Budget = 50% of $12,000 =	$6,000
Advertising Budget = 50% of Show Budget = (Includes everything spent to attract exhibitors and a public audience)	$3,000
Non-Advertising Budget = (Includes everything else)	$3,000

Examples:
· Site rental
· Portable toilets
· Secretarial services

- · Telephone calls
- · Complimentary food and ribbons for vendors
- · Identifiers for volunteers (shirts, ribbons, badges, etc.)
- . Entertainment
- . Sanitation Services
- · Postage

PROFIT = 50% of $12,000 =   **$6,000**

We have no idea how much you will actually have to spend on the items listed. We only know how much we've spent doing a show similar to the one described in the example.

The reason we can't give you a hard-and-fast set of numbers relates directly to our first rule of finance:

DON'T PAY FOR ANYTHING YOU CAN GET FOR NOTHING!

Solicit for goods and services. Use your creativity. Enlist volunteer assistance. Do you know someone with a small printing press, a computer, a copy machine, graphic art skills, free access to a community building or park? Prevail upon them.

What can you offer in return? Acknowledgement in your program? Future business from your club or organization? The chance to become involved in a worthwhile community venture?

Remember, you won't get what you don't ask for. You'll be surprised at how many people will be happy to contribute free or reduced-cost goods and services if they feel it is in support of a worthy cause. So, give folks an opportunity to help you. You won't be sorry.

Gate Fees and Admission Charges

By charging an admission fee, a show promoter is able to spread the financing of the show to all participants - public as well as exhibitors. When admission is free, all revenue must come from the exhibitors.

Charging a small gate fee can make possible lower booth fees, provide more money for advertising, and yield a higher profit margin.

For example, a very small gate fee of $2.00 can generate several thousand extra dollars in income with little risk of driving prospective customers away. But some caveats are in order.

Value For the Dollar

It would be hard to justify a gate fee, no matter how minuscule, unless you were offering something besides the selling of arts and crafts. People might not be willing to pay admission to a crafts-only show, but if there were other enticements such as entertainment, interesting food, and a festival atmosphere, a dollar might seem like a real bargain.

Admission fees, coupled with good entertainment, serve to keep people at a show longer, hopefully spending more time and money in the craft area.

Cost versus Benefit

If your show is indoors, controlling public entrance is a relatively simple matter. In most cases, a person or two at the front door collecting the money and making change is about all that is needed.

On the other hand, charging admission at an open, outdoor show will be a lot more difficult. The area may have to be fenced in or roped off, or patrolled, with all people being directed to one or two manned entrances. Sometimes, this is a lot more trouble and expense than it's worth.

One Last Point

As a neophyte show promoter, you may be reluctant to charge admission to an unproven event. This is a realistic attitude. You may be more comfortable offering a free-admission show at first and considering a gate fee later on, when your show is established, successful, and sure of attracting a good following.

In any case, remember that it is an option open to you, and consider it during your planning and organizing activities.

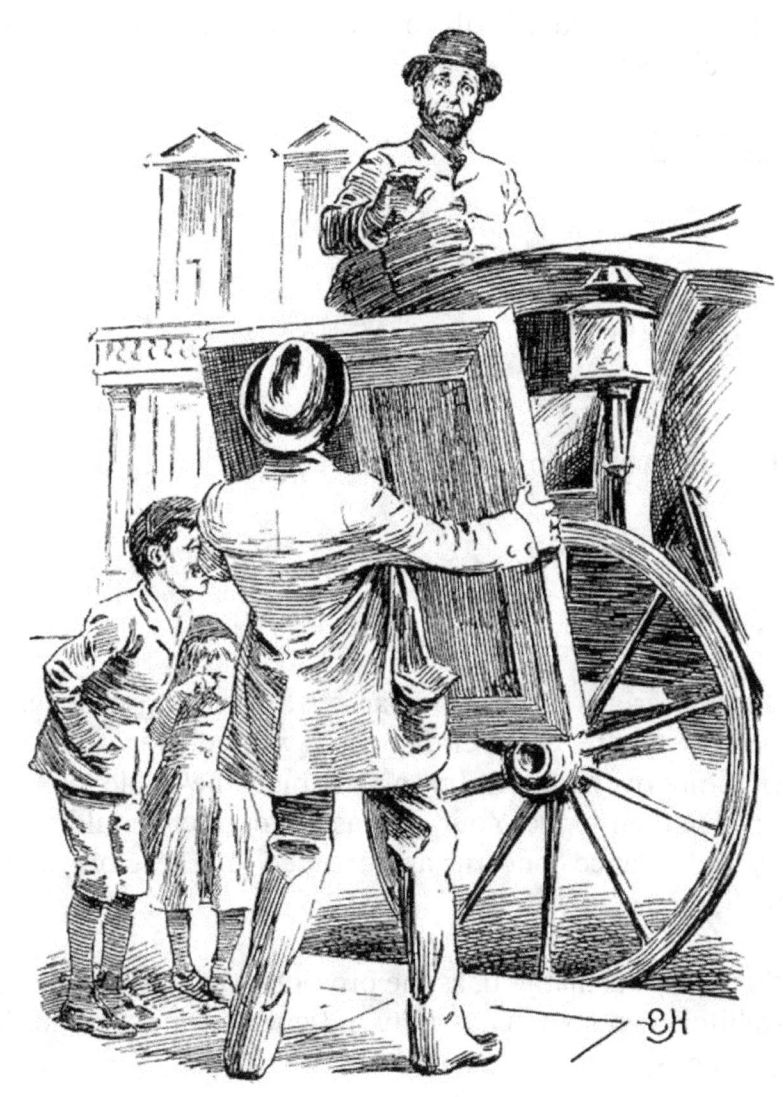

PART 2: Shaping The Show

Establishing Exhibitor Guidelines

Art and craft shows run the gamut in terms of quality. At the low end are open shows which often resemble flea markets. Quality is not an issue and anyone with the booth fee can enter. At the high end are invitational art shows and well-established festivals where competition is keen and only the best artists are chosen to show their work. Most craft shows fall somewhere in between.

QUALITY ANALYSIS

OPEN

Unjuried anyone can enter

JURIED

Selecting the 'best' from a group of applicants

INVITATIONAL

Pre-selection of exhibitors

If you want to attract serious professional artists to your show, better not promote a flea market type atmosphere. Good craftspeople will not want to be involved in shows filled with imports, junk jewelry, plastic machine-made toys, and other cheap goods which devalue their work. Your goal as a promoter should be to mount a show in which quality and balance concerns are attended to. Therefore, some type of jurying system will be needed.

Basically, all this means is that you, as the promoter, will ask to see some examples of potential exhibitors' work so that quality judgments can be made. Jurying can be done with photographs, slides, or original items.

For a first-time show, we suggest that you request three photographs of the work and one of the display set-up, if available. This will allow you to see what the craft item looks like as well as how the craftsperson presents his work to the public.

After you have put on a successful show or two, you may want to change your jurying requirements to slides and set up a panel of experts to participate in the jurying process. But don't make things too complex the first time out!

To deal with balance issues, we find it best to use an all-at-once jury date instead of admitting exhibitors as they apply. Unless you are looking at all applications at the same time, you'll have little control over balance issues. A show that has 40 jewelers, 10 potters, 20 tee-shirt booths, and very little else is not going to be enjoyed by many people, and the jewelers will be very unhappy that you have set each of them in direct competition with 39 others.

Even a well-rounded show will have more of some crafts than others, and that is perfectly all right. After all, there are many more jewelers and potters than scrimshaw artists and metal sculptors. And, although most people don't own a great number of sculptures, almost everybody has multiple jewelry or pottery items.

Your final balance will depend on which craftspeople apply to your show and the types of crafts represented. So don't lock yourself into exact mixes or quotas until you see what is available to you.

Attracting the Exhibitors

There are three good ways to find exhibiting craftspersons for your show: attend other arts and crafts events and invite skilled artists to apply to yours; blanket your area with press releases several months before your show; and place ads in the trade papers and magazines which are read by the artists you wish to attract.

One of the compelling reasons for taking six months to a year to plan a show directly relates to attracting exhibitors. Many of the best artists and craftspeople fill their schedules months in advance. You will be competing with other promoters for the most talented of these individuals. If you give yourself enough time to attend shows in your area and talk with the artists, you'll have a much better chance of attracting good people for your own show.

Be prepared to provide craftspeople that you contact with an application form on the spot and to offer concrete information about your show. At the same time, ask the artists which trade papers they regularly read. This will give you some ideas on where to advertise for other exhibitors.

Press releases that appear in local papers will be seen by local artists. Hopefully, your excellent copy will entice many locals to write for an application blank. (See Part Three.)
Be aware of the trade papers available in your area and place ads for exhibitors.

The Paper Trail

You will need a number of form letters for corresponding with potential and actual exhibitors, including the following:

- **Application Form**

- **Acceptance Letter/Confirmation** (including a map to the show)

- **Rejection Letter**

- **Show Day Letter** (including space assignment/map of the show)

- **Thank You Note**

Examples will be found at the end of this section.

The Application Form

An application form should contain all the information a potential exhibitor needs without being over-long or confusing.

Start off with a brief description of the event; proceed to event data (dates, times, location, cost, booth size, deadline, jury date, etc.); and conclude with a mail-in portion to be returned with the entry fee and photos for jurying.

Requesting a self-addressed, stamped envelope from the applicant for mailing your response is a great time and money saver, and we highly recommend it.

Acceptance Letter

Once you've selected the exhibitors who will participate in your show, it's time to mail acceptance letters. Try to get these out at least four weeks before the show date. Respect your exhibitors by not keeping them waiting until the last minute to hear from you.

The acceptance letter should include directions to the show (a map is a good idea), set-up times, and special rules to be followed such as unloading procedures and parking regulations.

Rejection Letter

Rejection letters should go in the mail as soon as the jurying process is completed. Give rejected applicants enough time to schedule another show and prevent a weekend of lost sales.

If the reason for the rejection was not one of quality, but because a category was filled, you may offer to place the exhibitor's name on a waiting list in case of a cancellation.

Show Day Letter and Space Assignment

On the day of the show, provide a letter which welcomes exhibitors, directs them to their spaces, outlines procedures to be followed, reiterates rules and regulations, and indicates who to contact with problems or questions. Explain clearly and simply. Try to eliminate confusion. A good letter will do much to control set-up chaos and set a positive tone for the morning chores.

Thank You Note

Some people consider "thank you" notes to be optional. We disagree. Courtesy is never optional.

From a business standpoint, if your show is successful, you will probably want to repeat it. Sending thank you notes to your exhibitors makes them feel positively toward you. At the same time, you can request their inputs for improving future shows and invite them to participate. You may even want to include an evaluation form on which each exhibitor can rate his/her experience anonymously. This type of feedback is worth its weight in gold!

Application Form

Come join us for a glorious day of fun in the sun as the
Parents' Club of Anton School presents...

THE HILL VALLEY SPRINGTIME CRAFTS FAIR

Sunday, May 19, at Bay Meadow Park

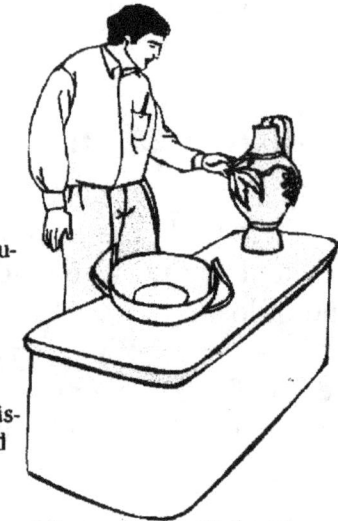

Surrounded by the foothills of Glorious Mountain, beautiful Bay Meadow
Park will be the site of a Springtime Crafts Fair which will offer the community an opportunity to view and purchase quality arts and crafts in a
setting of unsurpassed beauty.

Proceeds from the Fair will benefit the Drama and Music Departments of
Anton School. Entertainment will be offered throughout the day, and a
variety of quality foods and beverages will be available. Extensive advertising in the surrounding towns should assure a good-sized crowd of art and
craft buyers.

Requests for entry must be accompanied by 3 photographs representative of the work to be displayed
and the $50 entry fee. All work must be designed and executed by the displaying exhibitor. No im-
ported or mass-produced goods will be permitted. Each exhibitor will be expected to arrive at the
show with a professional booth display not to exceed 10'x10'.

Deadline for entry is March 15. Jurying will be completed on April 1, and applicants will be
notified of the results by mail no later than April 10. Please apply as early as possible. Entries in each
category (jewelry, pottery, wearable art, etc.) will be limited.

‒ ‒ Detach and mail to: The Hill Valley Springtime Fair • 2732 Council Crest Drive, Eastland CA 90909 ‒ ‒

NAME _____

ADDRESS _____

CITY _____ STATE _____ ZIP _____

PHONE (_____) _____ RESALE LICENSE NUMBER _____

CRAFT OR MEDIUM _____

Booth Size: 10'x10'   Cost $50 & 10% over $200

Enclose: ☐ $50 check payable to "Hill Valley Springtime"
              ☐ 3 photographs of your work *(labeled with your name and address)*
              ☐ a long, self-addressed, stamped envelope

I certify that the accompanying photographs are representative of my own work. I agree to be responsible
for my display at all times. I understand that all reasonable care will be taken but that no responsibility for
loss or damage is assumed by the Springtime Crafts Fair Committee, its officers, or agents.

_____   _____
Signature   Date

Acceptance Letter

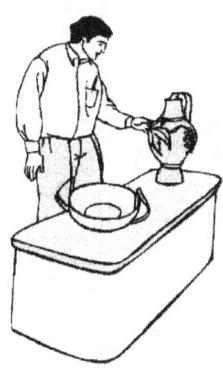

**The Hill Valley Springtime Fair
2732 Council Crest Drive
Eastland, CA 90909**

Dear

We are pleased to tell you that you have been chosen to participate in the Springtime Crafts Fair.

Set-up will be from 7 AM to 9 AM, Sunday, May 19, at Bay Meadow Park (See enclosed map). The show will open at 9:30. Failure to appear by opening time may result in forfeiture of your space.

When you arrive, please check in at the information booth to receive your space assignment and an envelope for commissions on sales over $200. You will also receive a coupon for complimentary coffee and a Danish, as well as a red Exhibitor's Ribbon. This ribbon will identify you to the public and allow you priority service at the food concessions.

Please unload quickly and park in the designated vendor parking area. Your booth must remain open until the fair closes at 6 PM.

Your space will accommodate a 1O'xlO' booth. You are required to have your tables covered to the ground and to sell only those crafts that were juried into the show.

Jurying photos will be returned to you at the end of the day when you turn in your commission envelope.

If you have any questions, call Dianne at 916-555-1234, weekdays, between 9 and 5.

Congratulations, best wishes, and see you at the Fair!

The Springtime Fair Committee

The Hill Valley Springtime Fair

Rejection Letter

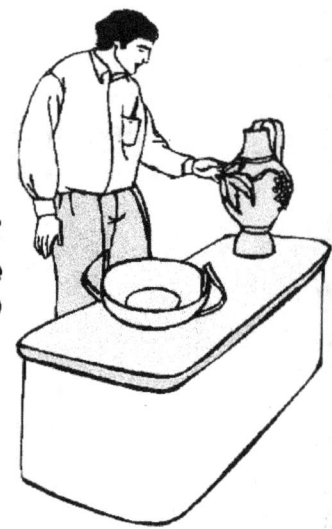

The Hill Valley Springtime Fair
2732 Council Crest Drive
Eastland, CA 90909

Dear

Thank you for applying to the Hill Valley Springtime Crafts Fair. We appreciate your interest and support.

Due to the large number of applications received, we regret that we will not be able to offer you a space this year. We do hope you will apply again next year.

Enclosed are your photos and check. Again, thanks for your interest.

Sincerely,

The Hill Valley Springtime Fair
Jurying Committee

Show Day Letter

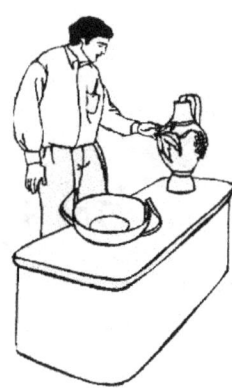

The Hill Valley Springtime Fair
2732 Council Crest Drive
Eastland, CA 90909

Dear Exhibitor,

Welcome to the Springtime Crafts Fair. We are delighted that you could join us and will do everything possible to help you have a rewarding experience.

Your booth space is highlighted on the enclosed site map. Please use the indicated street space for unloading and then move your car to the designated parking area before setting up. Volunteers in green tee shirts will be available to assist you.

Your booth must be set up by 9 AM and should not be taken down until the show ends at 6 PM. Tables must be draped to the ground and bags, packing materials, boxes, etc. must be kept out of sight. Please keep your booth tidy and dispose of trash in the appropriate receptacles.

Only the handmade craft items juried into the show are to be displayed in your booth. Violation of this rule will be cause for removal from the show and forfeiture of all fees paid.

Volunteers will make frequent booth stops to answer questions and provide assistance. Please let them know if you require assistance. The information booth near the front entrance will also be open during show hours for your convenience.

Have a great day!

The Springtime Fair Committee

Thank You Note

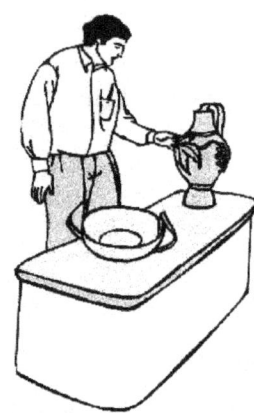

The Hill Valley Springtime Fair
2732 Council Crest Drive
Eastland, CA 90909

Dear

Thank you for helping to make our first Springtime Fair a success!
Working together, we produced a community event which was
enjoyed by a great many people and is sure to attract even more
attention in future years. We hope you found the day to be a fun and
profitable experience and that you will want to join us again next
year.

Please let us know if you have any ideas on how the show could be
improved in the future. We value your opinions and would be happy
to hear from you with any suggestions or comments.

Best regards,

The Fair Committee

A Word About Jurying Photos and Slides

Photographs and slides of exhibitors' work are often treated quite disrespectfully by promoters, especially inexperienced ones. It is very upsetting to artists and craftspeople to have their valuable jurying materials mistreated or lost, so take care to safeguard these items, and return them to their owners in good condition.

Jurying materials should always be returned with rejection letters. Some promoters also return photos with acceptance letters to save postage, but you might want to retain these until the show is over. Retaining the photos or slides allows you to check booth contents against items juried into the show in case of a dispute (an example: A potter who has been accepted on the basis of his decorative hand built sculptures suddenly displays several shelves of slip-cast ceramic figurines.)

Photos can be returned at the end of the show or enclosed in the thank you note sent out as soon as the show is over. In any case, let the artists know when they can expect the return of their materials.

What About Themes?

Does your show need a theme? Not really, but it's certainly something to consider. Themes can be a great source of publicity.

California is one state well-known for theme fairs and festivals. Californians celebrate almost every fruit, nut, vegetable, and flower grown in the state, as well as assorted mammals, reptiles, fish, and invertebrates. There are also festivals to honor famous people, several inanimate objects, and even a bothersome weed (The Poison Oak Festival)! Several festivals carry combination themes (The Peach Festival and Rickshaw Race, for example).

Beyond these options, fairs and festivals can also celebrate important community events (birthdays or founders' days), historical periods, ethnic groups, seasonal occurrences, and holidays.

A theme need not be serious or even completely rational. There is often a sense of whimsy and fun in these themes, traits which may be very appealing to the public. But there is also the real possibility that, given too many options (entertainment, food, parades, children's events, races, etc.), the public will eat, drink, and be merry without doing much craft buying. And this is death to your craftspeople as well as your hopes for attracting artists to future shows.

If you do decide on a theme, make sure that other available events attract the public but do not detract from crafts buying. Always play up the crafts fair sale aspects in your ads.

Entertainment

Consider including entertainment as part of your crafts show. Entertainment, when utilized, should support and enhance the crafts fair, but never overpower or detract from the main event which is, of course, the appreciation and sale of crafts. This means that some thought should be given to matters of scale and aesthetics. Obviously, what is appropriate to a large outdoor show will not work in a church basement.

Three basic categories of entertainment are:

STAGE (Bands, Vocalists, Dancers, Demonstrations),

WANDERING (Minstrels, Magicians, Storytellers, Jugglers, Mimes), and

CHILD-ORIENTED (Face Painters, Balloon Vendors, Puppeteers, Play Areas).

Stage Entertainment

Stage Entertainment generally takes place in a fixed area (stage) and can include bands of all types, vocal groups, dancers, and various demonstrations. (We've seen martial arts, skateboard, and dance/exercise demonstrations, to name only a few.)

Some show promoters use stage entertainment, particularly musical groups, to justify public gate fees and to attract a larger audience. Unfortunately, the people who are drawn to loud rock groups or the rowdier types of stage entertainment are often not the people who are interested in buying arts and crafts, so some discretion is needed. Avoid loud, teen-oriented entertainers! An audience of bubble-gum rockers will probably not buy very much art.

If stage entertainment is utilized, do not make it continuous. Several sets, 20 to 30 minutes long with at least 30 minutes between acts, encourage people to shop for awhile, then take an entertainment break, and then shop some more.

If you're using several acts, a master of ceremonies (MC) is a good idea. The MC warms up the audience, introduces the acts, and generally keeps things moving along.

COMPENSATION: It is possible to spend a great deal of money on entertainment. It is also possible to provide quality and variety without spending much at all.

Obviously, professional bands and/or vocalists must be paid. At a recent crafts fair with which we were involved, stage acts were paid $60 for a one-half-hour set, regardless of the number of performers in the act.

In contrast, amateurs are often eager to perform for fun and for the exposure it affords. Most communities have a ready supply of good amateur talent. Places to look include local schools for the performing arts (dance, voice, dramatics), college and community choruses and instrumental groups, skills courses (martial arts, gymnastics, aerobic exercise), and so on.

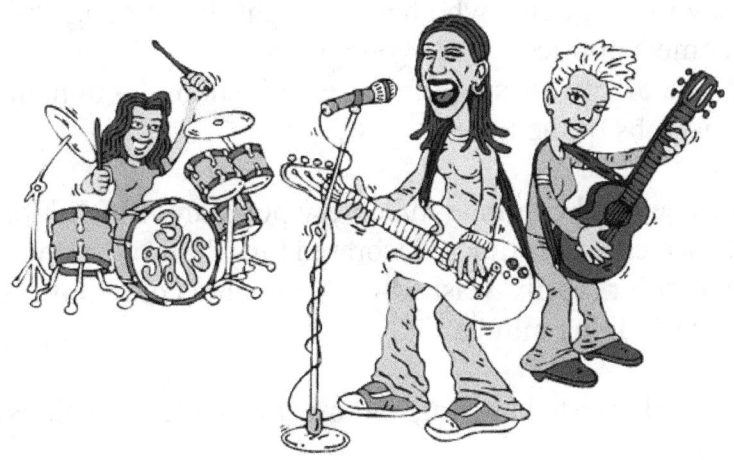

Wandering Entertainment

In the Middle Ages, troubadours or minstrels walked among the European townsfolk singing ballads of love and chivalry, usually to the accompaniment of a harp or lute. A kinder, gentler type of entertainment!

Wandering talent, be it a guitar-playing singer, a juggler, a mime, a storyteller, or someone else equally interesting, can be used very effectively in craft shows. Generally, such acts perform for a time in one spot and then move on to another location. The performer never stays too long in one place. Audience and actor are free to come and go at will.

Craftspeople tend to like this type of entertainment very much. It brings a part of the show to them to enjoy, delivers the crowd, and is not so loud that conversations with prospective customers are impeded.

COMPENSATION: Many wandering acts perform at shows on a "pass the hat" basis. They receive donations directly from the audiences they entertain. While promoters will still need to set guidelines for these performers (where, how long, how loud, etc.), they will not have to be directly involved in compensation issues. A nice plus for people who already have quite a lot to do and think about!

Child Oriented Entertainment

Many craft buyers will be parents who have brought their young children to the show. Providing some activities for the youngsters is good business. It pleases the parents, entertains the offspring, and allows serious shopping unhampered by the whines, shrieks, and sobs of the bored.

Face painters have been and continue to be very popular with children. We recently attended a show at which a beautician decorated kids' hair by spraying it "punk-style" with stripes of vivid color (easily-washed-out vegetable colors, of course). The kids loved it and the parents didn't mind a bit.

Balloons (helium-filled, twisted animal, and other air-filled novelties) are always popular fair items.

Children also enjoy "sidewalk" puppet shows or the informal amusements that they encounter while accompanying their parents through the fair.

Parks containing playground facilities can be good craft show settings. Parents can leave the kids at the swings, slides, and sandboxes while they browse and shop.

COMPENSATION: With child-oriented entertainment, compensation issues are mixed. Generally, balloon vendors and face painters should pay you a fee, as do crafts and food vendors. Sidewalk entertainers will probably be compensated by passing the hat.

In summary, the important questions which must be asked and answered when planning entertainment for your show are:

Will this entertainment
- attract people to our show?
- enhance selling activities?
- be appropriate to the show setting?

If you can answer these questions affirmatively you've probably made some good entertainment choices.

In Praise of Contracts

In the "old days" we dealt with all entertainers on a rather informal basis. ("Have your group here at 9:30. You'll do two sets lasting a half-hour each - one at 10 AM and one at 2 PM. We'll pay you $80. Okay, Guys?")

After a couple of "misunderstandings" and more than a little agony, we abandoned the casual approach and adopted a more professional contract-for-services system. After all, a crafts fair is a small business; there's no reason to be shy about acting in a businesslike manner.

No matter what types of entertainers you use at your show (and that includes the pass-the-hat wanderers), stipulate in writing what is expected and what will be given. In the case of the wandering acts, be sure to include the areas where performances will be permitted and the length of time the performers may remain before moving on (usually about one-half hour).

Food and Drink

Because a crafts show is at least a day-long event, some thought must be given to meeting the basic needs of audiences and exhibitors. Food is elemental. People need it, want it, and will leave the area to get it if it's not available on site. Beyond that, food and beverage concessions are proven revenue-producers.

Fairs and festivals provide edibles that range from simple to complex, from ghastly to glorious. There are several available options.

In-Place Concessions

If you decide to rent a large public space such as an exhibit hall or convention center, you may find that a concession stand is part of the deal. Some public facilities have a regular food supplier who has the contract for all events occurring within that hall. This arrangement has both positive and negative consequences.

On the plus side, you will not have to be involved in food planning. It will all be done by others who are professionals and should know the ropes. But there are also a few minuses. If the concessionaire only supplies a limited menu (soft drinks, coffee, hot dogs, and pastries, for example), that's what you, your exhibitors, and the public will be stuck with. If the food is not very good, you've got nothing to say about it. Also, there is no way for you to profit from the food or beverage sales, which is a major drawback.

Independent Food Vendors

Many large outdoor shows choose to deal with food the same way they deal with crafts. They solicit food vendors, charge them an entry fee and/or percentage of their sales, and provide an area at the fair for food services.

The pluses here are that the public can be offered a greater variety of interesting foods, and that revenue is generated for the promoter through fees and percentages. Because food booths tend to generate larger profits than crafts booths, fees charged are usually higher for these vendors.

Doing It Yourself

Because of the great potential for profit, you might want to consider running a food and/or beverage concession yourself. To do so, you will need to decide on which products to sell and to obtain the proper permits.

Offerings at your concession can be simple or elaborate. In any case, call your county health department for copies of the regulations relating to "temporary food facilities."

To protect the public safety, these regulations are very specific, and all temporary food facilities must have authorization to operate prior to the event.

The sale of alcoholic beverages is also tightly regulated and will be discussed shortly.

Local Organizations and Other Amateur Options

If you are not interested in running your own food or beverage concession, other community groups may be. PTAs, scout troops, fraternal organizations, booster clubs, etc. are often interested in being part of a community event that provides an opportunity for a little fundraising.

Beverages

Participating groups pay you a fee and/or percentage, just as professional food vendors would, and generally realize a tidy profit for their own organization's treasuries. It is usually a winning situation all around.

Obviously, some food concessionaires will also offer beverages, but beverage concessions can also exist on their own. Beverage concessions offer high profit margins from very little work, so again, you might want to keep at least one soft drink/coffee concession for yourself.

Soft drinks can be purchased in two ways - by the unit (can or bottle) or in bulk (large containers with a fountain requiring on-site preparation). Cans and bottles, while more expensive per serving, offer two advantages. Unopened containers can he returned for a refund at the end of the show, and on-site labor is minimal. However you choose to purchase your products, a soft drink concession is easy to run, can be very profitable, and is usually very popular with fairgoers, especially at hot-weather, outdoor shows.

Alcoholic Beverages

If you decide to consider beer and/or wine at your fair, the first thing to do is to check with local regulatory agencies to see if it's feasible. The sale of alcoholic beverages is heavily regulated. Rules and fees differ from state to state and county to county, so check with your local alcoholic beverage control agency for the specifics in your own area. A telephone number can usually be found in the State Government section at the front of your telephone book. You can also check with the county clerk or your local congressperson's office if you have trouble locating a phone number.

Following are examples of state regulations in three of the largest states - California, Illinois, and New York - during 2005 and 2006. Other states may have similar licensing procedures. Note: Getting the information may take more than one phone call and a bit of persistence.

CALIFORNIA

CONTACT:
State office in Sacramento (916) 419-2500 to get the telephone number for the local office (county) of the Alcoholic Beverage Commission Department.

NAME OF FORM:
"Application for Daily On-Sale License"

RESTRICTIONS:
Tax-exempt organizations only
FEES:
$110 per day for a License to sell beer & wine (special event)

ILLINOIS

CONTACT:
Illinois Liquor Control Commission 100 West Randolf Street Ste. 7 Chicago IL 60601

NAME OF FORM:
"Application for State of Illinois Special Event Retailer's Liquor License (Not-for-Profit)"

RESTRICTIONS:
Not-for-profit corporations only

FEES:
$25 for "Special Events Permit"

NEW YORK

CONTACT:
A.B.C. Boards - District Office 84 Holland Avenue, Albany, NY 12208

NAME OF FORM:
"Application For Temporary Beer and Wine Permit"

RESTRICTIONS:
Non-profit groups Only Beer and Wine must be purchased from a wholesaler.

COST: $26 plus $10 filing fee for each permit

If all of this sounds quite restrictive and complicated, the facts are not as bleak as they appear. For example, in California, the "tax-exempt organizations only" restriction can be circumvented by working with a liquor-licensed caterer. So, if you want to offer beer and wine, there is probably a way it can be arranged. As to the matter of whether you want alcohol at your crafts fair - let's examine the issues.

Some organizations would not think of holding a fair or festival without offering alcoholic beverages for sale. Certain holiday celebrations (July Fourth, Memorial Day, and Labor Day, for example) seem almost to demand it. And, not incidentally, the potential for profit seems too great to pass up.
Other organizations have little or no interest in offering alcohol no matter what the inducements. Opinions vary and can be based on a wide variety of financial, health, moral, and emotional concerns. Relative to crafts fairs, two beliefs seem to prevail.

1. Alcohol can loosen people up, making them more likely to spend money on crafts.

2. Alcohol increases the incidence of bad or rowdy behavior, which can have a negative impact on everyone involved with the show.

To Serve or Not to Serve

Which is the correct belief? Well, you know your town and you know your neighbors. Wine and Mozart will probably produce different results than beer and heavy metal! Alcohol in itself is probably not going to influence most people one way or the other. That's about all we can say. The decision is yours.

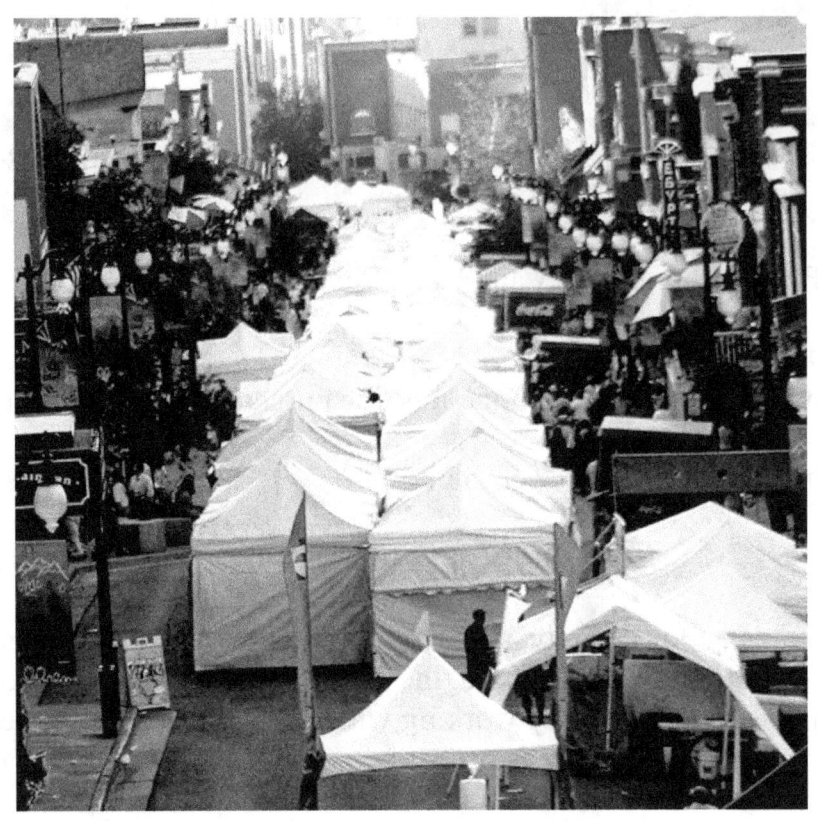

Park City Art Festival, Park City, Utah

PART 3: Attracting an Audience

Advertising & Publicity

"What if they have a crafts fair and nobody comes?"

This question is always on the minds of the artists you will be trying to attract to your show, and it should be on your mind, too. No matter what else you accomplish - a visually gorgeous show with wonderful arts and crafts, great entertainment, and terrific food - if you don't get the crowds out, you've failed as a promoter.

Nothing does so much to enhance reputations as the ability to deliver a buying crowd. So let's talk about designing a winning promotional campaign.

Presenting Your Show to the Public

The public will learn about your show mainly through advertising and publicity. There are differences between the two. Advertising means those messages which you pay the media to run, exactly as you have prepared them. You have complete control over the content. Publicity means the media take more responsibility (and control) for the content, but you don't pay for the coverage. Generally, you get more credibility from publicity, more "selling" with advertising.

Plan to spend about 50 percent of your show budget on advertising costs. Then get busy and generate as much local publicity as you can.

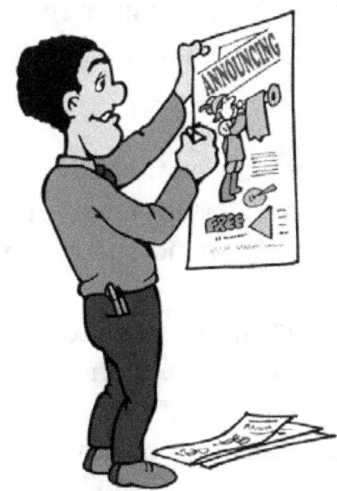

Designing the Advertising Campaign

Newspaper Ads

Your community is probably served by at least one general-interest newspaper and one or more community weeklies. Start your campaign here. The initial object is to reach as many people as you can within a radius of 15 to 20 miles of your show. Newspaper ads let you reach a large audience for a reasonable expenditure.

Your print ad should be attractive, large enough to be noticed, and written to include all the information a prospective fairgoer will need to attend your event. Keep in mind those Five Ws of journalism - who, what, when, where, and why - when writing your ad copy. If your show is in a place not well known to many people, consider dealing also with the journalistic H - how. For example, ads might include a small map with directions to the show.

If you're not charging an admission or gate fee, be sure to note this in your ad copy. "FREE ADMISSION" is a powerful incentive for many people. If you are charging admission, consider offering a discount to people who bring the ad to the show. This will accomplish two things: it will let people know they're getting a bargain, and it will also encourage them to clip out and save your ad.

How you develop your print ad will depend on a number of things. If you're working alone and have limited knowledge of, interest in, or talent for ad development, you might want to solicit the services of a graphic artist, talented friend, and/or typesetter. If, on the other hand, your organization contains a membership of varied talents and skills, look for someone who owns a computer and loves to play around with graphics.

If neither of these options excites you, lots of small newspapers will work with you to assemble your ideas into an effective ad. Obviously, the more work you can do yourself, the less money you'll need to spend and the more you'll get to keep.

After you've spent time, energy, and money developing a good display ad, you'll want to make certain that your messages reach the public at the times they will have the maximum impact. Newspaper ads might run two weekends before, one weekend before, and, once more, on the day before the show to refresh people's memories. Place display ads in as many local newspapers as your budget allows.

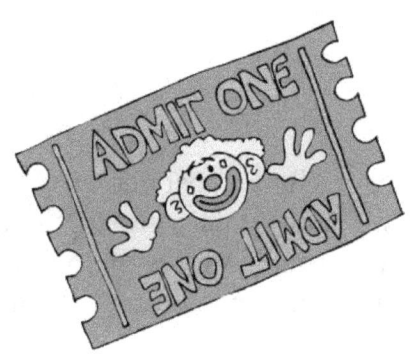

Newspaper Ad

actual size

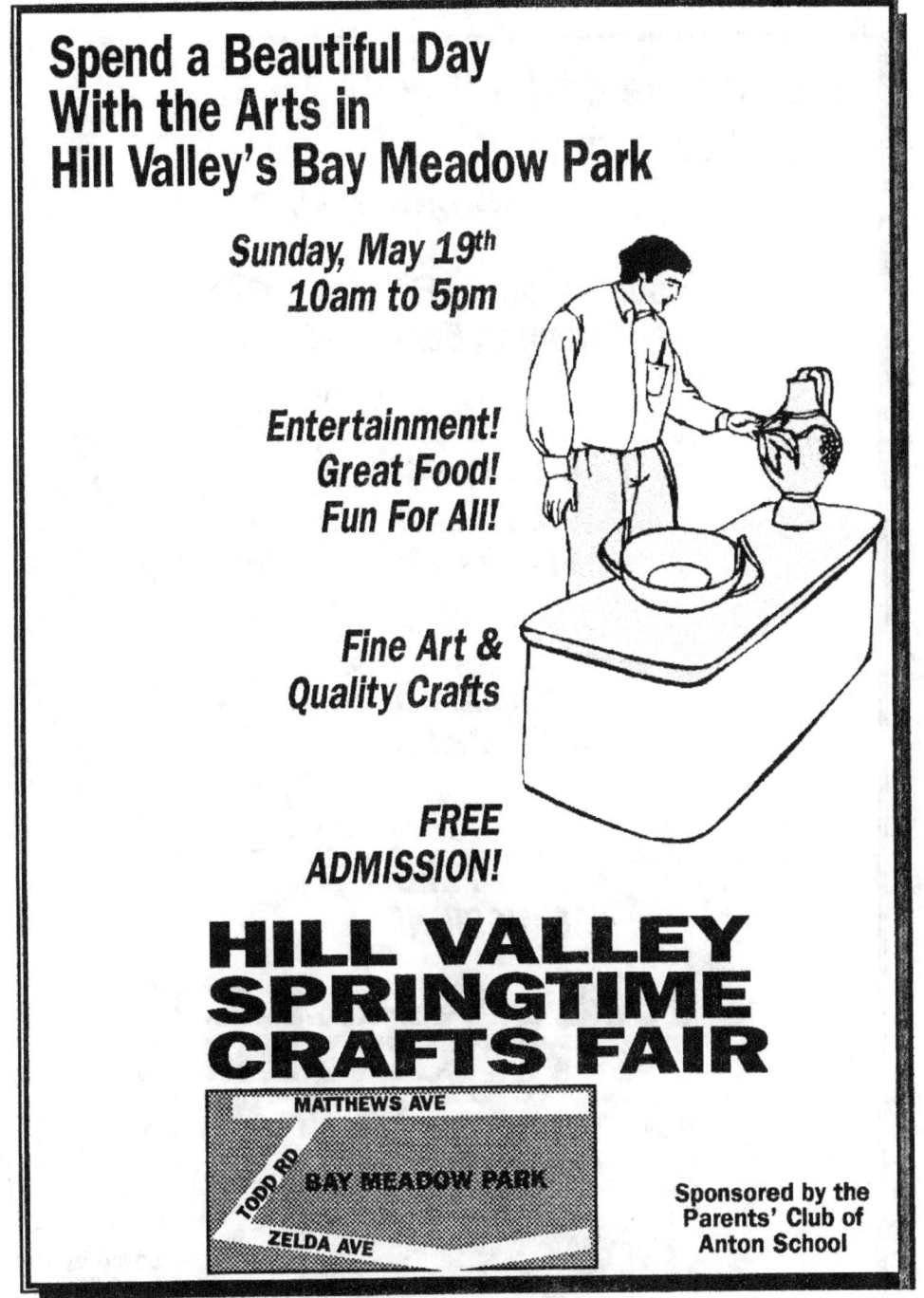

Spend a Beautiful Day
With the Arts in
Hill Valley's Bay Meadow Park

Sunday, May 19th
10am to 5pm

Entertainment!
Great Food!
Fun For All!

Fine Art &
Quality Crafts

FREE
ADMISSION!

HILL VALLEY SPRINGTIME CRAFTS FAIR

MATTHEWS AVE

TODD RD

BAY MEADOW PARK

ZELDA AVE

Sponsored by the
Parents' Club of
Anton School

Poster

Posters

Posters placed around town in the windows of local businesses and tacked to community bulletin boards and the like can be an inexpensive and very effective means of advertising.

Good sizes are 8 1/2" X 11" or 1 7"x 22". These are standard paper sizes. If your posters are too large, store owners will be reluctant to place them. Smaller 8 1/2"X 11" sizes work well on community bulletin boards, telephone poles, and other neighborhood posting places.

In designing your poster, consider simply enlarging your newspaper ad to poster size. Alternatively, art teachers or their students at local high schools and colleges may be willing to help you with your design.

Strive for a simple, uncluttered design that stresses the important facts (particularly what, when, and where). People will be reading your poster "on the fly" as they hurry past and will not bother to note a cluttered, information overloaded offering.

Color works to attract the eye. If your budget is large, you can have your poster professionally printed in three or four colors. For more modest budgets, basic black graphics on colored paper can be just as eye-catching for a great deal less money.

Pre-Printed Postcards

Postcards with a reduced version of your show's poster on one side can be sent in batches to each exhibitor a few weeks before the show. Professional exhibitors keep mailing lists of past customers and good business contacts. These postcards act as special invitations for each exhibitor to use when contacting a preferred clientele.

Banners

Placing an outdoor banner across a well-traveled street can be another way to advertise your show. However, the trouble and expense of this advertising method may be more than your group wants to handle for a first-time show.

Professionally made banners can cost up to several hundred dollars. This cost becomes less of an issue if the banner is used many times to promote an annual event.

If the banner is to be hung between utility poles or affixed to overhead wires or cables, permits will have to be obtained from the local utility company. Placing the banner will also require some assistance (possibly from the fire department), and the job must be done right, lest the banner fall down and become a traffic hazard.

Another simpler way to use a banner is to place one between poles or on buildings on or near your show site two weeks prior to the event. This type can be made by group members and will be much less expensive and much easier to cope with. Just make your banner large enough to be seen by passing motorists, and don't forget to secure whatever permission is required before placement.

Signage

On the night before the big event, plan to put up road signs directing the public to your show site. Simple black letters on a white background work quite well. All you need is a couple of words and a directional arrow (CRAFTS FAIR→). Make sure your signs are large enough to be seen from a distance by passing motorists.

Don't forget to check with the police department or city hall regarding local ordinances. If ordinances are very restrictive and won't allow you to put signs where you think they'd be effective, consider using "car signs." With this method, you can place your "CRAFTS FAIR→ " on top of an auto or truck and simply park the vehicle where it will be seen!

Electronic Media

Your group will probably not be able to afford paid radio or television spots (at least not the first few years!), but there are still ways to get your message on the airwaves - which leads nicely into our next topic.

Generating Publicity

Remember that publicity differs from advertising in that, while you do not have to pay for publicity, you do not exercise as much control over its content as you do with paid ads.

Because of this fact, good publicity can do a great deal to sell the public on your show. People know you've paid to advertise in the newspapers, and that you can say whatever you want. But a good article about your show appearing in a local newspaper is worth its weight in platinum.

Newspaper Articles

Sometimes you can use the placement of a paid ad as a way to maneuver for unpaid publicity. Local newspaper editors are always looking for human interest stories and interesting local events to cover. Why not give them some?

The Press Release

A press release is the vehicle by which you deliver information about your event to newspapers, magazines, radio, and television stations. Although the form may differ slightly from medium to medium, you will always want to:

- Type the information, double spaced, on one side of 8 ½"x 11" white sheets of paper.

- Answer journalism's Who, What, When, Where, Why, and possibly How questions in your text. As articles are often tightly edited due to space or time constraints, include the most important information in the opening two paragraphs.

- Include the name, address, and phone number of your group's contact person on the release.

- Check spelling, punctuation, usage, and form. Don't send off a sloppy piece full of typos, misspellings, or badly-worded sentences. Produce a professional-looking piece of work. Some people feel that it doesn't matter how these pieces are put together because it is an editor's job to fix things up. Don't believe it!

- Find out the correct name and title of the person to whom the release should be sent. Make a few phone calls to ensure that your press release gets to the proper editor or department. Otherwise, your efforts to get your materials read and used may amount to nothing.

Consider preparing several different releases. For example, several months before the show, use a press release in local papers to encourage exhibitors to apply to your show. Later on (one to two months before the show), send press releases with information slanted toward the fairgoing public.

Try to develop some personal contacts during the process of getting out press releases. It is most helpful to be on "telephone terms" with an editor or two. Editors are just like the rest of us and may be more kindly disposed to assist persons with whom they have some type of relationship. Such relationships are well worth cultivating.

Human Interest Pieces

In the process of planning your craft show, you will come in contact with newsworthy craftspeople producing unusual or unique craft items to which the public should be introduced.

Contact a local newspaper editor (perhaps one with whom you have established a relationship) and "pitch" a story. Have someone or something specific in mind. Editors don't respond well to vague notions or wishy-washy ideas.

For example, you might select a local craftsperson with an interesting background and an unusual craft ("Retired Air Force Colonel Produces Hand Carved Music Boxes with Love," or "Local Banker Custom Designs Dolls That Look Like Their Owners"). A skilled craftsperson who has won many design awards would be another good choice. Or a person who became a craftsperson in an unusual way (" Artist's Trip to East Africa Inspires Development of Synthetic Ivory Jewelry," or "Widowed Mother of Four Turns a Hobby Into a Business") might make a good subject for an article.

Begin negotiating human interest pieces several months in advance of the show. This is one time when you will need to be selective. Whereas general press releases will go out to as many sources as you can think of, a specialized article should be offered to only one newspaper or magazine at a time. Editors are not pleased when they see the piece you've given to them appear in a competing paper.

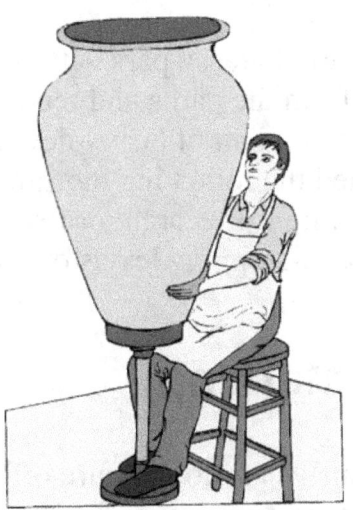

PART 4: Directing the Show

The Day (or Evening) Before

Marking the Site

Your most time-consuming day-before task will be preparing the show site for set-up. How you do this will depend on the site type (indoor/outdoor) and terrain (gym floor, grass, dirt lot, sidewalk, etc.) You will now be translating your previously-constructed floor plan from paper to actual site.

Floor Marking

After measuring off spaces on an indoor surface, you can use masking tape to mark the corners. Space numbers can be written on 3x5 cards and taped to the floor.

Field Marking

Grassy fields and parks or dirt surfaces can be measured off and marked by nailing 3x5 cards at the corners of each space and writing the space numbers on the same cards. Use arrows to designate which number corresponds with which space.

A few years ago, we tried to mark a grassy park setting by using a football-field chalk-stripe marker borrowed from the parks and recreation department. A brilliant idea, we thought! Unfortunately, a night of heavy dew completely obliterated all our beautiful lines, and chaos ensued the following morning at set-up. So ... it is probably best to avoid powdered chalk, lime, cornstarch, or flour for marking grass or dirt, unless you enjoy living with heart-stopping levels of uncertainty.

Street or Sidewalk Marking

Street or sidewalk shows are fairly easy to measure off and mark. Here, you can safely use chalk to designate space divisions and write a number in each space.

Floor Plan

After marking off your site, post your floor plan at the check-in area. You will also distribute this information to each exhibitor along with a welcome letter on the morning of the show. (See site map on page 53)

Signage

Now is the time to get road signs and vehicle signs in place. Send volunteers out to place signs along incoming roadways at previously decided locations. Don't wait until the last minute to decide how many signs you'll need or where you'll place them. With a good plan, you'll get this job done with a minimum of stress and grief.

Remember that signs will have to be removed promptly after the show is over. It is easiest if the persons placing the signs are also made responsible for removing them.

Comments about the Layout for the Hill Valley Springtime Fair

As you can see on the next page, The Hill Valley Springtime Fair was set up in Bay Meadow Park. Note that an information booth has been placed very close to the main entrance. The booth will serve craftspeople as well as members of the public.

Crafts booths are arranged to allow unimpeded traffic flow and to encourage attendees to walk around the park visiting booths as they go.

A few portable toilets near the craft booths have been designated for craftsperson's' use. Other public toilets are located a short distance away.

Food booths are in a separate section. Since food booths generate noise, grease, smoke, and trash, craftspeople appreciate such separations. Several trash cans have been placed in the area to keep garbage problems to a minimum.

The main stage is located far enough away from the crafts booths so that the sound level won't be intrusive, yet close enough to keep people nearby, even when listening to the entertainment.

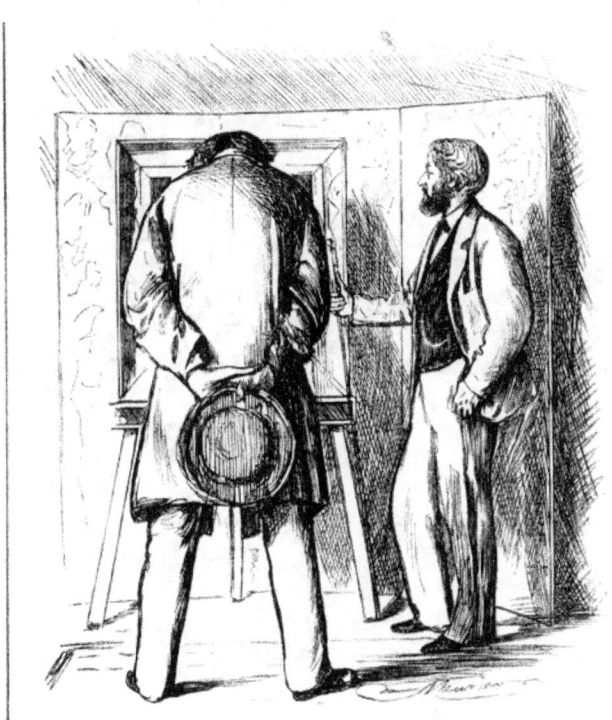

Layout

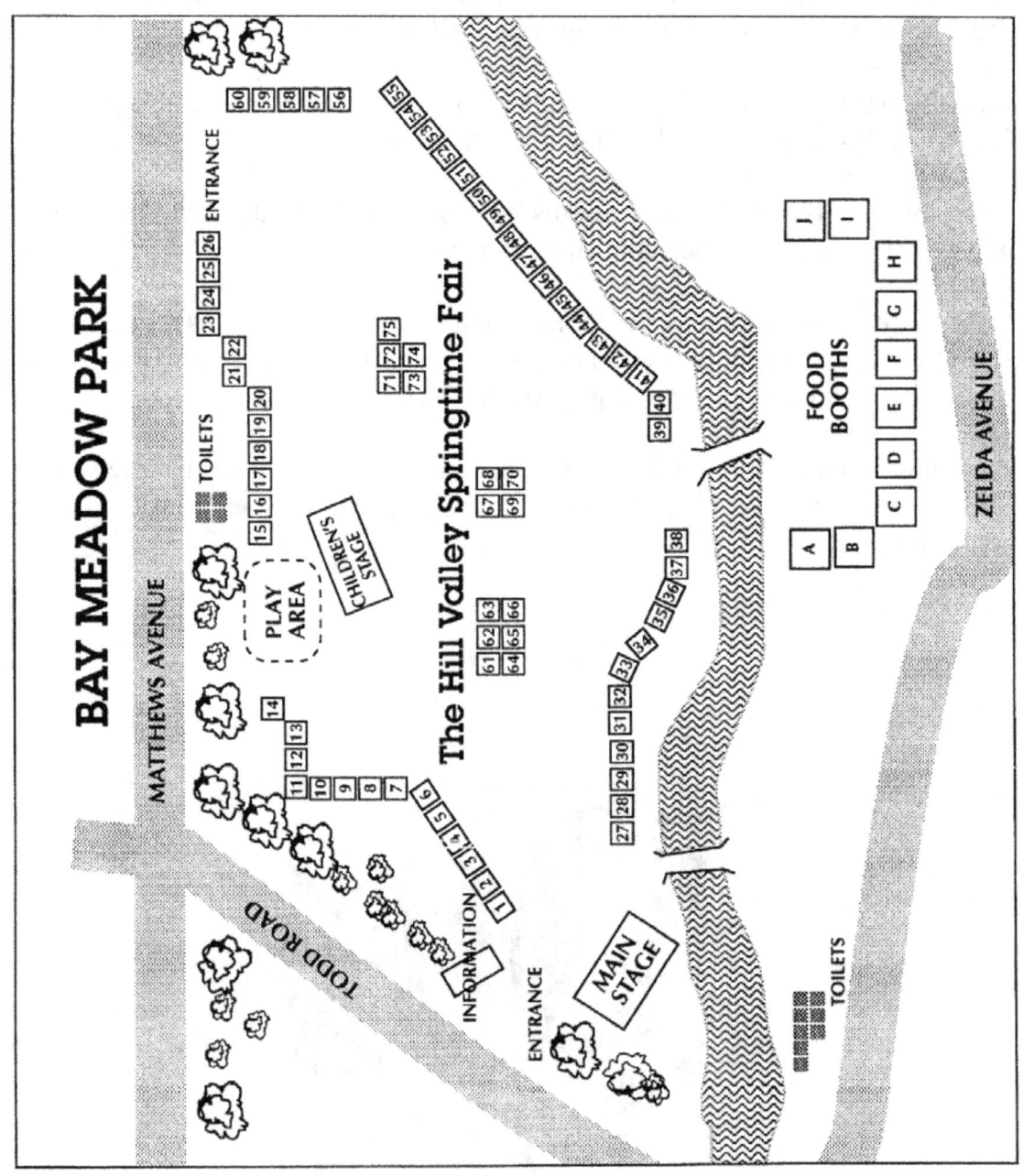

Showtime!

Setting Up

Plan to arrive at the show site with your staff one hour before set-up begins. Then, if anything unforeseen has happened during the night, you'll be there to fix it. (Remember our nail-biting experience with the chalk lines disappearing in the dew!)

Get your information booth or check-in table organized with exhibitor packets containing the show day letter, directions to the booth site, and any special items you've prepared (food coupons, exhibitor ribbons, etc.).

Post a large map at the check-in area so that visitors to the show can locate favorite exhibitors, and exhibitors can locate each other.

Provide as many staff members or volunteers as you can to help with unloading, set-up, and traffic control. Your object is to get everyone in place quickly with a minimum of confusion.

If you're putting on a large show, or if unloading space is limited, consider assigning staggered set-up times to your exhibitors. These times should be decided in advance and mailed to exhibitors along with their acceptance letters.

Plan to remain on site for the entire show. The importance of your involved, supportive, problem-solving, feeling-soothing presence cannot be overstated.

Be sure that you (or a staff member) visit every booth at least twice during the day. Wear a name badge or other identifier. Let everyone know who you are, and that you are available and interested. Take responsibility, and do your best to address small problems or issues before they become large concerns.

Booth visits will allow you to check to make sure that rules are being followed and that the items juried into the show are the items being offered for sale. Your physical presence alone will often be enough to discourage any would-be rule breakers.

Photographs

Oh, yes. One last thing. Don't forget to bring your camera (or have someone else bring one) to take some pictures of the happy throngs enjoying the show. These photos can be used for next year's publicity and as part of the documentation materials you'll be compiling on this year's show.

Cancellations, No-Shows, and Desertions

Cancellations and no-shows are an unfortunate fact of life, so it's best to have a plan for dealing with them. One major reason that these are so problematic is because they can downgrade the look and feel of your show. Vacant spaces give the same impression that one gets in a shopping mall where stores are unoccupied. A little seedy, a little sad, and certainly not the upbeat, prosperous image you want to foster.

If you're planning a two-day show, make sure that each exhibitor understands that he is expected to set up on both days. For any length show, make it clear that booths must remain up and open until the show closes for the day. Deserters should lose their entry fees as well as the possibility of showing with you again.

Have a stated cancellation policy which offers no refunds for short-notice cancellations and no-shows. If possible, keep a waiting list of people who can be called to replace cancellations.

Think about how you will cover spaces left vacant by no-shows. No-shows are more difficult to handle than cancellations because you don't get any advance warning. There are several ways vacant areas can be eliminated.

Filling the Holes

It has been our experience that on show day one or two craftspeople will show up hoping to "get in." These might be people who were rejected initially, folks who aren't terribly organized about applying to shows on time, or people who just found out about the show.

Some promoters feel that accepting "strays" at the last minute is a cardinal sin. Others don't mind as long as the work looks okay and the prospective exhibitor has the booth fee with him.

You'll need to decide how you will handle this issue. If you do decide to accept "stand-bys," wait at least an hour after the assigned set-up time before releasing a space. After all, the original craftsperson may have been delayed by an accident or car trouble or some other emergency.

In no case should you accept substandard work into your show just to cover a vacant space. You do have other options.

One of these other options is to allow adjacent booths to expand into the empty area. Many craftspersons welcome extra space and know how to adjust their booths to fit multiple space requirements. Just make certain that the additional area is not going to become a storage area or "garbage dump."

The last and least useful option is to change your booth assignments around a bit. This is not always possible or advisable. Do not ask someone who has already set up to move!

However, if the vacant space is near the end of a row or on a corner, it may be possible to make some last-minute adjustments of a minor nature which will improve the look of the show. Be creative, but above all be sensitive to the needs of the craftspeople who are already set up. Don't punish the innocent for the sins of the guilty!

Amenities

Sometimes in the hurly-burly business of planning and directing a show, promoters forget or ignore little extras that mean a great deal to exhibiting artists. A savvy promoter will realize that taking care of the exhibitors is just good business.

Ignore the needs of this group at your own peril. Craftspeople talk, and if you abuse them, actively or passively, you'll have a lot more trouble attracting good artists to your next event.

Try to arrange most or all of the following.

- Provide special artist parking at a location convenient to the show.

- Provide help with loading and unloading.

- Provide complimentary coffee and tea in the morning during set-up. Offering fruit juices and some type of pastry is also a nice touch which is greatly appreciated.

- Provide booth sitters for craftspeople working alone so they can leave for a few minutes to use the bathroom or to buy food. (Some promoters even send volunteers to run errands and order food for the artists.)

- At large shows, establish priority food lines for vendors. This is particularly important if you are unable to provide enough booth sitters to cover everyone's needs.

- If you're using portable toilets, consider setting up one or two near the crafts area designated for craftspeople only. Likewise, at a large indoor show, you might be wise to designate some restroom facilities for the exclusive use of the exhibitors.

- Give craftspersons a chance to evaluate the show anonymously, in writing (See Evaluation Form) and pay attention to what they say. Their comments will help you to put on an even better show next time.

- Rely on your good common sense and spend some time thinking about the show from an exhibitor's point of view. It should be fairly easy to see ways in which a show might be made more pleasurable to its most important participants.

- Lastly, don't forget that your attitude will rub off. A calm, smiling, reassuring demeanor will do a great deal to smooth out any problems that might arise.

Evaluation Form

FAIR EVALUATION FORM

Please complete this form and return it to us.
No need to sign your name!
Thanks for your help.

	(BAD)									(GREAT)	

1. HOW DO YOU RATE THIS FAIR FOR SALES?   0   1   2   3   4   5   6   7   8   9   10

    1-A. *(Optional)* APPROXIMATE GROSS, TO THE CLOSEST **$100**

       0   1   2   3   4   5   6   7   8   9   10   12   13   14   15

         16   17   18   19   20   21   22   23   24   25   26   27

     28   29   30   31   32   33   34   35   36   37   38   39   40

2. HOW DO YOU RATE THIS FAIR FOR ENJOYABILITY? 0   1   2   3   4   5   6   7   8   9   10

3. WOULD YOU RETURN NEXT YEAR? ☐ YES ☐ NO ☐ MAYBE

4. COMMENTS ABOUT THE FAIR IN GENERAL: _____

_____

_____

_____

5. COMMENTS ABOUT THE PROMOTER: _____

_____

_____

6. WHAT IS YOUR CRAFT?_____

The Hill Valley Springtime Fair
2732 Council Crest Drive
Eastland, CA 90909

PART 5: Following Up

So ... the show is over ... but wait! You're not finished yet. The time to take care of post-show tasks is while events are still fresh in your mind.

Your immediate responsibilities after the show will be to:

(a) clean up the mess,

(b) settle any outstanding bills,

(c) calculate your profits,

(d) thank all participants,

(e) carefully document your experience, and

(f) begin planning your next event.

The first three items are self-explanatory. The last three warrant some discussion.

Thanking all participants

How you do this will depend on your attitudes, your resources, and your finances. At the very least, send personal thank you notes to everyone who helped you - friends, volunteers, community groups, and businesses that provided services, products, or discounts. We have previously discussed the importance of thanking the craftspeople.

Some promoters put on a post-show party for their helpers. Parties can be simple or elaborate, daytime or nighttime, indoors or outdoors whatever you choose. The object is to show your appreciation in a tangible way by providing an enjoyable event. You'll also get to talk with many people, solicit their suggestions for improvements, strengthen your network, and unwind a little.

Stay in contact with your assistants. This will assure their readiness to help you in the future. And the next time you put on a show, you'll have an experienced crew to work with!

Documenting Your Experience

Documentation should be an ongoing activity that begins during the earliest planning stages of your show. Don't try to depend on your memory or you'll lose an amazing number of details - and details are important.

Keep files (card or computer) on your exhibitors. Include addresses and telephone numbers. These files will be part of future mailing lists. Also develop lists of volunteer assistants and useful business and civic contacts.

Store all items that can be used again (banners, signs, marking stakes, ropes, chalk, secretarial supplies, etc.) and keep copies of all advertising and publicity items (newspaper ads, press releases, posters, fliers, photographs, etc.).

Planning Your Next Event

Keep detailed records of your income and expenditures. A simple single-entry bookkeeping system will work just fine. You don't have to take an advanced accounting course to keep good records, but you do have to remember to save receipts and write things down.

You'll need this information to measure your financial success. If you're doing shows for a non-profit organization, the treasurer will need a financial statement, and if you're an entrepreneur, you'll need the information for the IRS. So ... make things easy on yourself and document as you go along.

The first show is the hardest! Think of how much you've learned and how many valuable business contacts you've made. You're now in a position to use your knowledge and contacts to plan an even better show next time.

We wish you good luck, good fortune, and many good shows.

We'll look for you in our travels. Hope to see you out there real soon!

Appendix I

Online Applications

Applying online with digital images has provided both solutions and headaches to artists and promoters alike. Artists like the ease of applying online, but face the problems of preparing images and uploading them. They also fear increased competition from increased applications, as other artists apply who might not have if it was harder to apply. Promoters like the idea of replacing slide projectors and the ease of scoring, as well as the increased pool of talent to chose from. Here is the information that an organization based in Colorado (www.zapplication.org) provides to promoters:

What is ZAPP™

ZAPP™ is a one-stop universal online application system that allows artists to upload high-resolution digital images of their artwork and apply to participating art shows, festivals and fairs. This Web-based system also enables the staff of art shows to more efficiently manage their application, administrative and jury processes online. ZAPP™ has a clear advantage over other online application systems currently on the market.

Managed by the Western States Arts Federation (WESTAF), a nonprofit arts organization
leading the field in the development of Web-based technologies, the ZAPP™ system was informed every step of the way by input from artists and art show directors. Each of these voices contributed greatly to the system's development—from functionality to graphics. Through this collaborative process, the ZAPP™ team has created a system that is user friendly and efficient for both artists and art show staff.

ZAPP™ Benefits

Art shows that license ZAPP™ have access to a robust management system that conforms to their show cycle—from the application process, through jurying and even booth sales. All communications between shows and artists are facilitated and automated through ZAPP™.

Art show directors no longer spend time and money printing and mailing applications and mailing notification letters. Staff administrative time is significantly reduced.

Traditional slides and carousels are replaced by state-of-the-art digital equipment for the jury process. As a result, application, administration and jury processes become streamlined and efficient.

Benefits to Art Shows and Jurors:
- Little to no data entry and significantly lower mailing costs
- Application fees processed electronically
- Automated communication with artists
- Slides and slide projectors are replaced with high-quality digital images projected by LCD projectors via Roku digital media players
- No loading and unloading slide carousels; no jammed slides; no physical pulling of rejected artists' slides; no slide carousel rattle
- Roku's allow jurors to zoom in for image detail; images are always in focus and can be viewed at precise and simultaneous intervals
- Easy-to-use online forms for scoring
- Easy-to-build finalist list via reports generated after jury elimination process

Benefits to Artists:
- Using ZAPP™ is free
- Applications are completed and submitted in one online location
- Receive instant e-mail notifications with application status and
- other information
- Applications can be managed while traveling
- No more multiple paper applications
- Save money on postage and production of multiple sets of slides
- Jurors will view digital images of artwork with consistent projection quality
- Contact information and images are secure

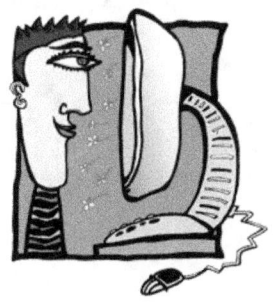

Appendix II

Resource List: Advertise Your Show

ACF News Post Office Box 476, Glenshaw, PA 15116 412-487-7715 Primary coverage: mid-Atlantic states and the Eastern Seaboard

ACN Showtime PO Box 104628 Jefferson City, MO 65110-4628 Primary coverage: Central States

Craft Digest PO Box 155 New Britain, CT 06050 860-225-8875 Primary coverage: New England and Upper East Coast

Craftmaster News PO Box 39429 Downey, CA 90239 562-869-5882 Primary coverage: Western States. Also publishes **The Crafts Fair Guide**

The Crafts Report 100 Rogers Road Wilmington, DE 19801 800-777-7098 Coverage: National

Island Craft Bulletin 110-D Leilehua Road Wahiawa, HI 96786 808-622-1049 Primary coverage: Hawaii

SAC 2120 S. Columbia Street, Bogalusa, LA 70427 800-825-3722 Coverage: National

Sunshine Artist 4075 L. B. McLeod Road, Ste E, Orlando, FL 32811 800-597-2573 Primary coverage: National

www.festivalnet.online Primary coverage: National

Appendix III

What Artists Want

Tips from Artists for Promoters (from www.craftshowplace.com)

1. Don't call us "vendors." Vendors sell hot dogs, imports. Call us artists. Everyone feels better. Art is special, vending is common.

2. Make spaces 10' 6". Every one gets a little wiggle room. It won't kill you.

3. Don't let artists set anything in front of their booth. No chairs, photos, plants, display racks, umbrellas, anything that messes with the flow of traffic to the booth next door.

4. No late hours on Fridays. People do not rush from work to buy art from a craft show. They come on Saturday.

5. More days. We need Fridays to make the booth fee. Artists with jobs who complain about Friday shows are taking opportunity from full-time artists.

6. Name tags. No tags with pins that destroy clothing. No tags on neck cords that dangle and get in the way. No wrist bands. Use a clip-on name tag holder.

7. Awards? Who cares. Put the money in advertising.

8. Have something for vegetarians at artist dinners.

9. Never charge artists extra for insurance. You can get it cheaper than we can. We don't need it. Our art doesn't hurt people. Charge food venders for insurance. Get a policy for the whole show.

10. Never cash booth fee checks before acceptance.

11. Ask for four slides and a booth shot. Not three, not five, not 10.

12. Deadlines are by post mark, not by "received by."

13. No items with tags or stickers that say "Made in another country." It doesn't matter who designed it and had it made overseas, it shouldn't be in a craft fair.

14. Musicians selling CD's in a booth must provide headphones, not use speakers. Or put them in a separate area. A booth is not a stage. It makes it hard for an artist next door to talk about their craft to their own customers.

15. Don't put artists next to a music stage where the music drowns out their conversation.

16. Apps are due 4 months before a show. Not 1 year, 8 months, whatever. We don't even know if we will be alive in a year, much less what we are going to be doing.

17. Leave artists alone when setting up and packing up. We know what to do, how and where to park. We know how to drive in and pick up our stuff, we do it every week. We can work it all out ourselves.

18. Don't take a big commission. Northwest shows are the worst. 20%, 25%, 30%!!! Forget that. If you want to support the arts, don't rob the artists.

19. Don't prohibit rugs or require them. Rugs save our products when they fall down, and make every one feel better. Same goes for awnings. Require that awnings be 7 feet high.

20. Indoor shows, turn up the lights all the way. Lots of light makes people happy. The darkened halls make people depressed.

21. Set aside a restroom or a few porta-potties for artists only, so we don't have a line.

22. At pack up, leave a few trash cans around. Many shows take up the cans before artists finish packing, and we have nowhere to put trash.

23. Make porta-pottie suppliers keep them supplied with paper throughout the day, provide a wash station, and keep it filled with water or hand-cleanser.

24. Digital applications are just confusing everyone. If you want to process and screen applications digitally, then you should be prepared to convert the artists slides to digital yourself..

Order books direct from Craftmasters!

A Beginner's Guide to Selling Your Crafts   ISBN 978-0-9655193-3-5 $29.95

Complete information on how to sell your creations direct to the public at craft fairs and art shows. Shows the best booth display for all weather use that draws people in to look and buy your work. Contains addresses and ratings for the best craft fairs and art shows across the US. Includes the best craft fair guides in the country, a list of show promoters who promote multiple shows, and a list of the top craft galleries around the country. Also has instructions for 14 spreadsheets and forms you can download for Microsoft Excel and Word. Includes instructions and examples for a craft pricing calculator, inventory tracker, mail list manager, business plan, invoice, show calendar, a form to organize our application deadlines, show expenses, and legal agreements for consignment, sales reps, and more. 244 pages.

Microsoft Office for Artists and Craftspeople   ISBN 978-0-9655193-1-1 $39.95

Over 70 templates and spreadsheets to help you organize your shows, price your products, keep your books, and plan your business. You need Microsoft Word and Excel to use these templates. Minimum software requirements for using the software templates included on the CD-ROM: Personal PC computer with Microsoft tm Windows Microsoft Office 2000 or newer or Word 6.0 and Excel tm 6.0 or newer. Not available in Mac format. 128 pages and CD-Rom

How to Put On a Great Craft Show   ISBN 978-0-9655193-8-0 $24.95

This is the book you have in your hands. Order copies for your organization, or to give to people you know who want to put on a craft fair. 70 pages

To order any of the above publications, send a copy of this form and a check for the total amount of the order plus $4.85 for Priority Mail shipping to Craftmasters, P. O. Box 1655, Sebastopol, CA 95473. California residents add 7% sales tax. Allow up to a week for delivery. MasterCard, Visa, and AMEX also accepted. You can also order online at www.craftmasters.com

Quantity	Title of Book	Price	Total
Name:		Sub-Total:	
Address:		Shipping:	$4.85
City, State, Zip:		California Tax 8%:	
Email:		Total:	
Phone:			
Card Number:		Expiration Date:	
Signature:			

Notes: